GATHERING LILIES
FROM AMONG THE THORNS

Finding the Mate God Has for You

TIM & BEVERLY LAHAYE

New Leaf Press

TIM &
BEVERLY
LAHAYE

THE
HEARTH
AND
HOME
SERIES

First printing: March 1998

Published in association with the literary agency of Alive Communications, Inc., 1465 Kelly Johnson Blvd., Ste. 320, Colorado Springs, CO 80920.

ISBN: 0-89221-368-X
Library of Congress Number: 97-75863

Cover by Left Coast Design, Portland, OR.
Interior illustrations by Pamela Klenczar.

Introduction

The most important decision you will ever make in life, next to receiving Jesus Christ as your Saviour, is who you will marry. For unlike most decisions you make, that decision, for good or bad, will affect everything else you do as long as you live.

Out of your marriage will come the children who will affect the first half of your life or more, and how you and your partner relate to each other will affect their lives, marriages, and even your grandchildren someday.

For that reason it is imperative that you start out right by finding the right partner. God has just such a person for you, and we have developed some time-tested principles for helping you find that person.

You will find those principles in this book. We know they work, for we have shared them with hundreds of young people who put them to the test and, besides, they worked for us. We just

celebrated our 50th anniversary — and looking back we can honestly say we wouldn't change a thing.

But some reading this book may say, "I have already missed God's will in finding a mate — why should I read it? That's easy. So you don't miss the "good or acceptable will of God" for your life (Rom. 12:2).

If you're single, no matter your age, you need to read this book.

— Tim LaHaye

Gathering Lilies from Among the Thorns

Did you know that life's most crucial decisions will be made between the ages of 18 and 25? During that time, you will be faced with many choices. Some will be minor decisions while others will have an impact on the rest of your life.

Suppose you impulsively purchase a car without putting much prayer or thought into it. If it turns out to be a "lemon," your poor judgment may simply result in expensive repair bills and a lot of inconvenience and aggravation. Since this was a minor decision, you eventually trade in your mistake without any lasting effect on your life.

Other decisions are not so easily dismissed. In fact, during the seven-year period between 18 and 25 years of age, you will make five decisions that will chart the course of your life.

How will you answer these five important questions?

Life's Five Most Important Decisions

1. What will I do after I finish high school?

The kind of school, college, or job you choose will set your life on a course that will likely determine the kind of education you receive, how much money you will eventually earn, and the opportunities you will have in the future.

If you decide to enroll in a vocational or trade school, you probably won't become an engineer, lawyer, or a teacher. If you choose to attend college, it's unlikely you will later decide to be a plasterer, plumber, or carpenter.

Your post-high school education — or lack of it — will affect your life's vocation. And that's your second great decision.

2. What career will I pursue?

Some high school graduates know exactly what they want to do in life and begin pursuing their college or career goals immediately. Others choose to join the military or get a full-time job before deciding on a specific course of action. Some feel that God is calling them to serve Him as a pastor, church music director, youth pastor, or missionary.

As long as you find the right training ground — and are available to God to make the right decision about what to do with your life — you will eventually be headed in the right direction.

3. Where will I live?

God has a will for where you live, including your state, city, and neighborhood.

You may choose to stay in your hometown or take a job in another state. If God calls you to be a missionary, you will probably live in another country far away from family and friends. In fact, that decision may take you to several countries during your lifetime.

No matter where you live, you can serve the Lord.

One of our family's greatest joys has been to pray for our neighbors and see them come to know Christ as their Lord and Saviour. That's one of the best ways we as Christians can further God's kingdom.

4. Where will I attend church?

It's not about *whether* you will go to church, but *where*? This is a question you should ask God, whether you live on a college campus, on a military base, or at home with your parents.

The Bible says, "Not forsaking the assembling of ourselves

together" (Heb. 10:25). You need the fellowship of other believers at every stage of your life.

God has a will concerning which church you should attend. If you are not regularly hearing the Word of God as part of your routine Christian experience, you will not continue to grow as a believer.

It is also important to find the right church. Look for a church where God is praised, the Bible is taught as God's Word, and Jesus is lifted up as Saviour, Lord, and soon-coming King. Then, attend every Sunday, get involved in serving your church family, and tithe your income.

5. Whom will I marry?

Don't think in terms of *will* I marry, but *whom* will I marry? I believe it is God's will for young people to marry. Whom you marry is a vital decision that will dramatically affect the course your life will take.

Finding a mate who will enrich your life and with whom you can enjoy spiritual, mental, and physical unity will be your most important decision. If you are married to the man or woman God has chosen for you, all your future decisions will fall pleasantly into place, as you seek His guidance.

If you put Christ on the throne of your heart and seek His will for your life, the choices you make regarding these five decisions will set you on the right course for the rest of your life.

Making Right Choices

Life is full of decisions. And making right choices is not easy. In fact, it's probably one of the hardest things to do in life. Why? Because there is a constant struggle between man's will and God's will.

1. Whom will you serve?

If your motto is: "I will do as I please," you are living according to your own will. You have chosen to ignore God's commands and have refused to place Jesus Christ on the throne of your life. As a result, all your decisions are based on your desires, your needs, and your ego.

Behind the scenes, another force is also at work. With great skill and cunning manipulation, Satan subtly tries to influence your decisions by pulling your will in his direction.

When God says, "Young man, young lady, give Me your

life," Satan counters with, "Don't waste your time calling on Jesus Christ."

Ultimately, however, the decision is yours.

2. Who controls your life?

Once you have trusted Him as Saviour, you must make another decision. Will you make Jesus Lord of your life? In other words, will you submit your will to His will? This is where the battle line is drawn — at the point of your will.

You can only be equipped to make right decisions by consistently making Christ Lord of your life. That's why it is harder to live for Christ than it is to die for Him.

Life will bombard you with decisions. You can make your decisions based on doing it "my way" — like Frank Sinatra — or you can choose "the perfect will of God."

God's Word commands:

> Present your bodies a living sacrifice, holy, acceptable to God, which is your reasonable service. And do

not be conformed to this world, but be transformed by the renewing of your mind, that you may prove what is that good and acceptable and perfect will of God (Rom. 12:1-2).

Why is God interested in your body? Because it is through bodies that He communicates His message.

If you're going to be "transformed," as the Bible says, you are going to be different. This is where the real test of your commitment to Christ takes place.

Don't be afraid to have different standards and principles. Don't worry about what other people think because you choose to dress modestly and refuse to go to nightclubs or R-rated movies. You can't live "godly in Christ Jesus" and still look and act like the devil.

Don't back off because you're different. That should be the hallmark of a Christian. The Bible calls us "a peculiar people" who are eagerly doing "good works." If you're

zealously serving Jesus Christ, that's all the peculiarity you need to be different from the world.

3. How can you find God's will?

> Do not conform any longer to the pattern of this world, but be transformed by the renewing of your mind (Rom. 12:2).

How do you renew your mind? By reading and studying the Word of God. That's how you will be able to test and approve what God's will is.

When you know and obey His will, you will find that it is not only "good" but also "pleasing." It pleases God, and it will be good for you. In fact, God always has your best interests at heart. His will invariably points you in the right direction.

As a young person with your life ahead of you, it's not too late for you to find and do "the perfect will of God."

How do you find God's will? Ask Him:

> In all your ways acknowledge Him, and He shall direct your paths (Prov. 3:6).

Finding the perfect will of God for your life is the formula for happiness. I have yet to find an emotionally frustrated person who is doing the perfect will of God. But I have met a lot of emotionally satisfied people who are living for God and seeking daily to do His will in every area of their lives.

God has a will for your life. Don't settle for anything less when deciding where you will go to school, what will be your vocation, where you go to church, and whom you will marry.

Lining Up with God's Will

It's exciting to make decisions when you have access to the Divine Computer — the storehouse of God's knowledge. After all, He knows the end from the beginning, and all you have to do is find His will.

Most people want the will of God for their lives revealed to them in advance. They say, "If you write me out a ten-year program — and I get a chance to look it over — if I like it, I'll do it."

God does not give us advance notice and instruction. Why not? Because He wants us to walk in the Spirit on a day by day basis. So don't be alarmed if He doesn't give you any more than one day's knowledge of what you should do at a time. He wants you to keep coming back again and again.

Whether it's a question of where to attend college, what career to pursue, or which girl or guy to marry — or whatever — if you acknowledge God by telling Him you want to obey Him, He will direct your paths.

How do you find God's will? Three areas should always be in alignment when you are seeking to know God's will: the Word of God, circumstances, and peace in your heart.

Keep in mind that it takes time for these three areas to come together in agreement.

1. The Word of God.

The Bible, the written Word of God, contains His laws, and outlines what He expects from us. His commands are not arbitrary or optional. They must be obeyed.

Suppose a guy were to ask me, "How would you like to go into business with me?"

And I said, "Fine, I've got some money I'd like to invest. What do you want to do?"

"Oh, I'd like build a tavern."

How much time do you think I should spend praying about that decision? I already know that the Bible says, "Wine is a mocker, Strong drink is a brawler, And whoever is led astray by it is not wise (Prov. 20:1).

How can I expect God to bless something He has condemned in His Word? God's leading will always be legitimately in accordance with His Word.

Jesus told His disciples:

> He who has My commandments and keeps them, it is he who loves Me. And he who loves Me will be loved by My Father, and I will love him and manifest Myself to him (John 14:21).

Jesus said, "You have my commandments."

How can you "have" His commandments? By reading, memorizing, and obeying the principles provided in God's Word.

A. Do what God has already told you to do.

If you're a rebellious Christian who is stubbornly refusing to regularly study the Bible, don't ask God to give you direction for your life. He won't. He reveals His ways as you obey Him. The more you are obedient, the more He leads you in the right direction.

Jesus has promised, "I will manifest myself to him." To whom? To anyone who keeps His commandments and who loves Him. In fact, that's how we show we love God — by keeping His commandments.

Many times people pray, "Lord, reveal yourself to me."

"I will," He replies. "Just do what I've already told you to do."

If we are not obeying the instructions He has given us in the Bible, God will not give further revelation.

Suppose you are asking God to send you a mate. You go to God's Word, which says, "But seek first the kingdom of God and His righteousness, and all these things shall be added to you. (Matt. 6:33). Yet, instead of seeking to promote the gospel, you spend all your spare time going to singles' bars in an effort to attract Mr. or Ms. Right.

Do you think God will answer your prayer?

B. Avoid basing decisions on "feelings."

Many Christians try to chart their way through life by feelings. Those who make decisions based on emotion or goose bumps are headed down a rocky road instead of a "straight path."

Whatever your plans or decisions, chart them by the Word of God.

A young Christian businessman who had been saved less than two years came to me for advice one day.

"I've been offered a fabulous deal — just a fabulous deal," he exclaimed. (I'm always suspicious of that word "fabulous.") "A guy wants me to go into business with him and merge our two printing firms," he told me. "He's 63 years of age, and in two more years he'll retire. Then I'll own the entire operation — his business and mine!"

"Why haven't you gone through with it?" I asked.

"I don't know. There's something that bothers me about it. I thought I'd come by and see you."

"Let me ask you a question. Is this guy a Christian?"

"Oh, he's a nice fellow — kind of religious, but he's not a Christian."

"Did you know that the Bible says, 'Be not unequally yoked together with unbelievers'?"

"Really?" he asked, and we looked it up together.

"I guess that settles it, doesn't it? If the Bible says 'don't do it,' I don't do it."

He phoned the man and said, "Sorry, I can't do it."

A week later, this young man phoned me and said, "You just saved me $40,000!"

Apparently this nice upstanding citizen, 63 years of age, had borrowed $40,000 on the equipment in his shop. He had planned to form this partnership, then take my friend's money and head for Mexico, leaving him to make the payments.

This young man learned a valuable lesson: If you want to live a productive Christian life, keep God's commandments and don't base your decisions on feelings. His commandments are not grievous.

When we need to make an important decision, we often think we are going to lose some fabulous opportunity or make some great sacrifice. In reality, we are merely operating by faith. In fact, I've never made a sacrifice for God in my life. Every time I face a difficult decision and choose to obey, I think, *I'm really sacrificing for God.* But He always turns it into a blessing.

If you determine to live your life according to the will of God as defined in His Word, you will never have any regrets.

2. Circumstances.

When determining God's will in some area of your life, the second point of alignment centers around circumstances.

Many Christians prefer circumstantial living, but circumstances are not adequate alone. Their importance in decision-making should not be overemphasized. Sometimes we make the mistake of forcing the Word of God to line up with a chosen set of circumstances.

> All things work together for good to those who love God, to those who are the called according to His purpose (Rom. 8:28).

Whenever you're seeking the will of God, read the Word regularly so the Holy Spirit can instruct you.

Don't be quick to act. Wait for the circumstances to line up

with the Word. Circumstances will fall into place and either close doors or open doors.

3. Peace.

God is the author of peace; He is never the author of confusion — unless you're going contrary to His will.

> Let the peace of God rule in
> your hearts (Col. 3:15).

The word "rule" comes from a Greek word that means "umpire." You know what an umpire does? He calls "safe" or "out."

That's exactly what peace can do for us. When God is the author of something in our lives, we have peace.

Girls, the most handsome Christian athlete on campus may have asked you to marry him. It seems the circumstances are lining up with God's Word. But if you don't have peace in your heart, watch out!

It's not enough to have only two of the points in line, you need all three. When they make a straight line, then you can say God is in it.

Let the umpire have the last word.

The Dating Game

Dating is a phenomenon of western civilization. In fact, two-thirds of the world today follows the same custom that was practiced during Bible times: Parents select the mate for their son or daughter.

I met a young man with a master's degree from Seattle Pacific College who told me how he met his wife. When he returned to his home country of India for a visit, his father said, "I've picked out a girl for you." Fortunately for him, his father was a born-again believer and had selected a lovely Christian girl.

"John," I asked, "When did you see your wife for the first time?"

"When she started walking down the aisle of the church."

Talk about a walk of faith! Yet, that is exactly what all marriages require. Once you make the decision to marry, that's it! You accept the life partner God has given you, and you walk by faith to make your marriage work.

Sometimes, I think, maybe we should go back to arranged marriages. It would make life a lot simpler. But I would probably be stoned for promoting such an idea.

Dating, however, doesn't have to be complicated, especially if you are a Christian, committed to following Christ and seeking God's will for your life. In that case, the Holy Spirit is your matchmaker. You only have to wait for Him to make a match!

In the meantime, I suggest you follow these simple suggestions.

1. Date only Christians.

What draws people together? Usually, it

is some common interest. That is often followed by physical or personality attraction that leads to association, and association leads to love. Love at first sight, however, is a myth perpetrated by Hollywood.

How can you avoid becoming emotionally entangled with an unsaved person?

Cut it off at the pass. If he or she is not a Christian, don't associate with him or her in an intimate or personal way.

Don't even pray about the will of God regarding someone who isn't a Christian. The Bible has already revealed the will of God: "Do not be unequally yoked together with unbelievers (2 Cor. 6:14).

Set this simple rule for your life: I will not date an unbeliever, and I will never marry an unbeliever.

Sounds simple, but it works.

"But look at all the fun I'll miss," you say.

How much fun can it be to date someone when you are constantly wrestling over the different standards by which you conduct your lives? He wants to see an "R-rated" movie, while you have always avoided ungodly entertainment. She sees nothing wrong with your spending the night in her dorm room or apartment, but you don't want to give the "appearance of evil."

A little compromise today always leads to a bigger compro-

mise tomorrow. If you start out compromising in little things, you'll be faced with great compromises. Sooner or later, you've got to take a stand. It is much easier to take a stand in the beginning when you know you're guided by the principles of God.

Whenever two people get together and one is a Christian and the other is not — whether it's on a courting basis or two fellows sharing a college room — one of three things will always happen:

A. The Christian will reach the unbeliever and lead Him to a saving knowledge of Jesus Christ. That's the best outcome.

B. The unbeliever will have a souring, deadening effect upon the Christian.

C. They will naturally lose interest in each other.

Either the unsaved person will rise to the

position of the Christian, and they will reach common ground, or the Christian will stoop to the level of the unbeliever, or they'll separate.

Why does it always happen this way? Because the unsaved person, "the natural man" cannot understand "the things of the Spirit of God, for they are foolishness to him; nor can he know them, because they are spiritually discerned" (1 Cor. 2:14).

2. Look for someone who can complement your particular temperament.

A quiet, intellectual young man who had been dating a bubbly, vivacious girl expressed his concern over their different personalities.

"I've taken a battery of psychological tests, and we're so different," he told me.

"Well, I could have saved you the money those tests cost you," I told him. "Of course you're different. I know the two of you are different. In fact, you're only strange when you're attracted to someone who is just like you."

After all, what is more different than a woman and a man? We are usually attracted to someone with strengths opposite to ours.

All of us are born with a certain type of temperament. Whether male of female, we all fall into one of four categories —

or a combination of two types:

> A. Choleric
> B. Sanguine
> C. Melancholy
> D. Phlegmatic

Temperament is not developed as you mature or imposed on you during your upbringing. You are born with it. However, your temperament can later be adjusted by the Holy Spirit.

Whenever I walk into the nursery in our church, I am able to identify the four personality types in the little children playing there.

The choleric children have all the toys.

The sanguine kids are running around having a happy time.

The melancholy children are looking around, staring at everyone.

The phlegmatic kids are off in the corner playing all by themselves, not bothering anyone.

During the dating years, you will probably be attracted to another person of the opposite sex in an affectionate way for reasons you don't fully understand. The first infatuation may be because of looks, appeal, circumstances, or biological magnetic attraction.

Also at work is a subconscious attraction toward the strength we admire in that person — strengths that correspond with our weaknesses.

I've never known anyone to consciously say ,"I fell in love with Mary because I am an uninhibited, disorganized sanguine and she is a meticulous, careful, and neat melancholy." But that's exactly what happens.

At the same time, neat, precise Mary is attracted to sloppy Fred because he's gregarious and outgoing. But they don't realize it!

Two sanguines would never fall in love because a sanguine is always on stage performing and needs someone to be his audience.

Two cholerics would never even go on a date. Why? Because they would chew each other up before they left the house.

Two melancholys probably wouldn't marry because they would both get disturbed at the other's morose disposition.

Two phlegmatics would never marry because they'd both die of old age before one got up enough nerve to ask the other.

One couple in our church could have been married four years sooner if she'd just gotten around to asking him. He's a phlegmatic engineer, and she's a choleric nurse. They went together and went together and went together.

Finally, she said to him "Are you ever going to ask me to marry you?"

"Well," he answered, "I've been thinking about it."

"For how long?" she asked.

"About four years."

That conversation finally precipitated some action. He asked her — with a little coercion on her part — and she's been leading him ever since!

Rocky Choleric will usually fall in love with Polly Phlegmatic. Why? She's the only one who can put up with his hard-driving dynamic personality.

After marriage, however, Rocky may turn into a caustic, cruel, sarcastic, unaffectionate character if the Holy Spirit does not get hold of him. And Polly's sweet, demure, gracious, gentle, quiet spirit can turn her into a stubborn, sullen, silent, and disorganized wife.

By being aware of the strengths and weaknesses of the different personality types, you can ask the Holy Spirit to change those areas in your life that need His touch. You can also begin to pray that God will begin now to prepare the temperament of the person He has for you — so you can both complement one another.

3. Date for fun, not marriage.

Some guys approach dating much too seriously. You're afraid if you ask a girl to have cappuccino with you, she'll be planning the wedding before your cup is empty.

Girls, when a guy asks you out for the evening, don't think you're making the greatest commitment of your life. You're sim-

ply committing yourself to him for one evening, and he's committing himself to you to be a Christian gentleman. That is all; nothing more. Don't go home afterwards and start browsing through *Modern Bride* magazine.

Christian girls should be choosy. If you are walking closely with the Lord, your greatest fear should be marrying outside of God's will. Unless you know from God he is Mister Right, don't even entertain the thought of marriage.

Guys, if you meet a girl you'd like to get to know better, why not enjoy a nice, sociable evening together? Let's face it, there's something exotically inspiring about being in the company of the opposite sex. And it's worth that 20 bucks you'll invest in refreshments.

My advice to young men and women: Lighten up! Enjoy each other in a casual relationship and have fun while you're dating.

4. Relax and trust the Holy Spirit.

If you're walking in the Spirit regarding your male/female encounters, you can relax and enjoy dating — or not dating.

Remember, it's the Holy Spirit's job to work everything "together for good" in your life. He picks the time, the person, the circumstances. When you are ready, and your prospective mate is prepared, the Holy Spirit will let both of you know at the same time.

Girls need to keep in mind that some guys are simply not interested in dating. It's not that they aren't attracted to the opposite sex, it's just that they have a lot of other things on their minds.

Our society puts a lot of pressure on men to "be all that they can be." Many guys — and girls — take their lives and futures seriously. Between the ages of 18 to 22, however, a guy is more likely thinking about finishing his education, getting a job, and pursuing a career. His life is indefinite and his future uncertain. Until everything falls into place, marriage may not be high on his list of things to do.

At the same time, a fellow may be afraid to date for fun. Most Christian guys try to be considerate of a girl's feelings and don't want to mislead them. Guys feel guilty if they want to date but have no intention of marrying at this point in their lives.

My suggestion to fellows in this situation? Relax and let the Holy Spirit put the process of natural selection to work. The cream will rise to the top in any milk bottle.

On the other hand, God is not the author of confusion. Whenever you are tense or pressured or confused about a dating relationship, you can be sure that the Holy Spirit is not in control. You need to back off, take time to pray, and seek the counsel of wise believers who know and love you.

Any person God sends into your life will bring with him or her a sense of peace, love, and joy. If he or she is the right one, you won't have to wonder. Your spirit will bear witness with the Holy Spirit that this is God's choice, and He will bring you together in His time and in His way.

5. Keep your dating relationship pure.

When I suggest that you date for fun, I'm assuming you know the difference between good, wholesome, clean Christian fun and an illegitimate "good time."

The world teaches that sex is okay as long as it is "safe." God's Word teaches that sex is okay as long as two people are married — and there are no exceptions.

If you want to keep your relationship wholesome, you must avoid the biological, magnetic attraction that the two sexes naturally have for one another. By making physical contact off-limits, you set your heart and mind free to learn more about each other in the mental and spiritual realm without the sexual distraction.

A woman wants to be loved for her person, not her body. That's why a man needs to get to know that real woman — not her body, but the person who lives inside the body. The Bible calls it "the hidden woman of the heart." Most guys don't even know this "hidden" woman exists because all they can see and think about is the physical woman.

When you go out on a date as a Christian guy and a Christian girl, you want to return home knowing you have conducted yourselves in a manner worthy of Christ. The best gift you can give your date is a peaceful night's sleep with a clear conscience.

In counseling sessions, I deal with people all the time who are suffering a backlash of guilt resulting from the sin they practiced during their dating years. Don't let that be the legacy you take into your marriage. It will only come back to haunt you.

6. Guys, conduct yourself as a Christian gentleman.

A girl respects a guy who respects her body and understands that she has a responsibility to God to keep herself pure. As a

A GIRL WITH
A LOVING
RELATIONSHIP TO
HER FATHER IS LESS
LIKELY TO GIVE
HER VIRTUE AWAY
BEFORE MARRIAGE.

Beverly LaHaye

Christian, you should treat her like a sister in the Lord. If you really love a young lady, you're going to protect her from doing anything that would cause her to sin against God.

Sure, I know you have certain driving forces within you. That's normal. In fact, God made you that way. But satisfying those needs should be reserved for marriage. Remember, one of the attributes of the Holy Spirit is self-control.

On a date, everything you do should please the Lord Jesus Christ — or you've got no business doing it. Just do one thing - what's right.

Be a man. Make it your goal to please one master - Jesus Christ — not the violent force of lust or passion or free love. With the help of the Holy Spirit, you can resist any temptation. All you have to do is ask.

7. Girls, learn to say, "No!"

Don't allow yourselves to be a victim of male lust. That's the world's concept — not God's will.

You have a Heavenly Father who loves

you and wants to protect your purity and virtue. Any spirit that leads you to violate the Bible's standards of modesty and sanctity is not the Holy Spirit.

"If I act too religious, I won't be popular with the boys," you may complain.

Guys have big egos, and they don't always keep confidences. As I remember, the boys in the locker room knew the difference between the girls who were trying to please the boys and the girls who had standards.

The girls who wanted to please the boys — and did — had lots of dates, but the girls who had standards were the ones who got married first. In fact, some guys will tell you anything and everything as long as they get what they want.

"You mean, I shouldn't trust my boyfriend?" No.

If you have to displease a fellow to please Jesus Christ, don't apologize. Don't even feel bad. If he doesn't understand that you'd rather please Jesus more than anyone else — then he's not the guy you want. The fellow God has for you will want you to please Jesus Christ. In fact, he won't respect you if you don't.

I know it's not easy, especially in our sexually promiscuous society. At times you will need tremendous discipline and be required to invoke a Holy Spirit-inspired "No!"

The stronger you are in the Spirit, the easier it will be to

resist the sexual pressures and temptations of dating. On your wedding night, however, you will rejoice knowing you kept yourself pure for the mate God gives you.

Happy is the young person who pleases Jesus Christ in dating.

8. Don't tempt the opposite sex with revealing clothing.

During one of my seminars, a young man handed me a piece of paper on which he had written this question: "I have a problem with a girl I've been dating. She wears very short skirts, and I'm not sure if the feeling I have for her is love or lust. Can I be filled with the Spirit and feel this way? Can she be filled with the Spirit and entice me like that?"

Many Christian women and girls do not understand the problem a man has with his eyes and his mind.

When I was in the Air Force, every barracks I went into had pictures of half-nude women. One day I was given the assignment of cleaning out the WAC's barracks — this was before the military became coed. After I finished my job, I realized I had not seen one picture of a nude man.

Women aren't stimulated by what they see in the same way fellows are.

Jesus pinpointed this issue when He said to men, "But I say to you that whoever looks at a woman to lust for her has already committed adultery with her in his heart" (Matt. 5:28).

The Lord Jesus knew what was in men, and He knows what's in women. Men have a problem with lust that women don't have.

Christian men want their eyes to be dedicated to God, but they are constantly bombarded by scenes that incite them to lust.

At the same time, Christian women and girls aren't much help. When a woman sitting in a church pew has her legs exposed far above her knees, such a sight is not conducive to a man's worship.

The apostle Paul wrote, "Therefore, if food makes my brother stumble, I will never again eat meat, lest I make my brother stumble" (1 Cor. 8:13). In other words, if my behavior or actions cause someone else to sin or to interfere with his relationship to God, then I need to change what I am doing.

Some girls may say, "Nobody is going to tell me what to wear!"

If you desire to walk in the Spirit and to please Jesus Christ,

then you need to obey God's Word, which says, "I desire therefore that the men pray everywhere, lifting up holy hands, without wrath and doubting; in like manner also, that the women adorn themselves in modest apparel, with propriety and moderation, not with braided hair or gold or pearls or costly clothing" (1 Tim. 2:8-9).

During a singles seminar, I was counseling a young lady in the dining hall when I looked across the room and saw several girls praying together. Above the table, everything appeared reverent. Below the table I saw everything that was immodest.

I looked back at the faces of the girls and realized they were oblivious to the show they were putting on. They were honestly sincere before God, praying and having fellowship with the Lord, but I am sure they would have been appalled if they had seen themselves from my perspective.

Short skirts are only part of the problem. Bikinis and other revealing clothing do not belong in the wardrobe of any woman or girl who is seeking to obey God's Word and serve Jesus Christ as Lord.

9. Pray together.

"Do you really think that young people can pray together when they are dating?"

You bet I do. In fact, the most beautiful relationship in the world takes place when two human beings of the opposite sex pray together.

"What should we pray about?" you ask. Pray about where to go and what to do.

"When should you pray together?" I suggest you pray a "shortie" at the beginning of the date and a "longie" at the end.

It's good to have a planned time to pray. Why? It's a safeguard.

In the beginning, you can pray and ask the Lord to help you please Him in all you do on your date. Then, if you know at the end of your date that you're going to have a time of prayer together, you will be conscious of where you go and how you conduct yourselves on your date.

If you can't pray together while you are dating, you need to reevaluate your relationship to one another — and to the Lord.

10. Avoid unnecessary body contact.

Every male and female has a biological, magnetic pull toward certain members of the opposite sex, but that doesn't mean he or she is the one God has chosen for you.

If she's your number, just being in the same car with her will make your ears come to a point and your temperature rise, but that's normal. That's the way God made you. In fact, that is a natural reaction.

Take dancing for instance. Any red-blooded guy and girl who stand close while moving their bodies together to the accompaniment of throbbing, mind-numbing rock music can't help but get turned on.

As for dancing in general, I would not consider it a wholesome practice for any believer who is striving to lead a godly, Christian life.

In fact, anyone who uses his or her body to sexually stimulate members of the opposite sex is tempting others to sin.

Unnecessary body contact only serves to pour gasoline on your emotional fires. It only takes one touch to erase your standards and toss your good judgment out the window.

I have counseled Christian girls who told me they were so sexually stimulated after dancing that they lost all control once they got alone in the car with their date.

In a moment of time, you can destroy your own self-respect and the respect of the other person.

Remember the story of David's son, Amnon, who forced himself upon his sister Tamar? After that moment of fulfilling his raw fleshly desire, how did Amnon feel? He despised Tamar. Why? Because he had no right to her, and the guilt of what he had done destroyed his overwhelming feeling of love for her. It was not the act; it was the way the act was performed. The illegitimacy of the function violated the laws of God that were written on his heart.

You see, we not only have the law of God, but we have a conscience that accuses us or excuses us.

Sex before marriage changes a couple's relationship forever. It is an extremely hard, if not impossible, to halt once started. Usually it removes the young man's motivation for marriage,

destroys their spiritual life, and most often ends up ruining their relationship and they break up. At best, even if they marry, they carry into their wedding bed the unnecessary baggage of guilt.

When you are together, be conscious that Jesus Christ is watching everything you do — and don't do anything that would displease Him. If you don't displease Him, you won't displease your parents or yourselves — and you won't have to look back on your courtship days with embarrassment and regret.

Don't risk destroying your relationship with guilt by allowing unnecessary body contact to incite your passions and tempt you to disobey God. Relaxed dating in a spirit-controlled environment will produce a wholesome relationship that you can both enjoy without guilt or shame.

If you led a sexually active lifestyle before becoming a Christian and are living with the guilt and shame of your past, I have good news for you. God's Word says, "Therefore, if anyone is in Christ, he is a new creation; old things have passed away; behold, all things have become new" (2 Cor. 5:17).

When Jesus Christ comes into your life, you become a brand new creature — the slate is wiped clean.

From this point on, keep your life pure and holy before God. Don't dwell on the past. Just be grateful you found Him in time. Rejoice that you have a new life and that your body now belongs to Him.

God's Way to Find a Mate

Your loving Heavenly Father is interested in every detail of your life. Most of all, He wants to be vitally involved in the process of choosing the person who will become your life's partner.

Finding a mate for life is serious business, and God has determined several important ground rules that will keep you on track. The Bible calls them "commands" or principles.

Secular educators have probably told you, "There are no blacks and whites in life; everything is in that nice gray zone."

That may sound cool, but such a philosophy leads to confusion and produces intellectual malcontents or psychotics. Why? Because without predetermined principles, making decisions becomes almost impossible. Simple decisions develop into extremely complex issues.

Have you ever said, "I just wish someone would tell me what to do!"?

I've got good news. The Bible deals in absolutes. God's Word says, "Thou shalt not commit adultery." That's an absolute.

One day a fellow came to my office and told me he was having an affair with his brother's wife.

"I know she's already told you about it," he said. "She's been feeling really guilty."

At that point, I realized he had not come for counseling but simply wanted to appease his conscience.

"You have to keep in mind," he continued, "that I'm in love with her."

I replied, "No, you have to keep in mind that you're committing adultery."

"No!" he shouted, "this is love."

"It's adultery!" I yelled even louder.

Finally, I shouted him down, but he was still unwilling to face the fact that what he was doing was adultery. Our society doesn't like to use that word anymore.

Remember, compromise never solves anything.

You have two simple choices: black and white. If you violate God's command, that's a black. If you face the temptation and don't give into it, that's a white.

Every time you meet an attractive member of the opposite sex, are you going to get all hung up on whether or not you should commit adultery?

In your lifetime, you will probably have many opportunities to have sex outside of marriage. If, however, you have decided to obey God's Word, you don't have to pray about what you are going to do when a tempting sexual situation arises. You don't have to reorient yourself or restructure your thinking patterns. The Bible says, "Thou shalt not!"

Happy is the individual who calls sin what it is. In this age of semantics, some people try to confuse the issue by putting new labels on old sins.

When a young woman told me she was all confused about the new morality, I replied, "It's not new. It's just plain old immorality. You know, situation ethics — if the situation calls for it, it's fine. If you go back to the Bible and situate yourself, you'll find the situation calls for marriage! There is no alternative."

Another young lady told me, "Well, it hasn't happened very often, but in this day and age, you know, you have to restructure

your thinking to get along with the new philosophy of free love."

"In other words," I replied, "you believe it's all right to commit fornication."

"Oh, now, Pastor LaHaye, we shouldn't call it that."

"Why not? That's what the Bible calls it," I said.

There is no gray zone in God's Word — only principles and standards. That's why it's so much simpler for Christians to make decisions. That's why Christians can make judgments and have definite, unwavering opinions about social issues.

Some people say, "Well, aren't you Christians an opinionated bunch!"

Yes. In fact, we're very narrow-minded. Why? Because Jesus Christ said it's a "narrow way." It's either Jesus Christ absolutely or not at all. If we are going to follow Jesus, we must obey His commands and the principles laid out for us in God's Word.

Let's look at several biblical principles regarding how a Christian should select a mate for life.

1. Only marry a Christian.

Whenever a young person says to me, "I would like your opinion on my marrying so-and-so," I always respond by asking, "Is so-and-so a Christian?"

If the answer is "I'm not sure" or "I'm praying for him or her," my guess is that the prospective partner is an unbeliever.

When you think about marriage, don't let yourself drift into a gray zone by playing mental footsie with the idea of marrying anyone who isn't a Christian.

If the person you are dating and considering marrying is an unbeliever, that can't possibly be the will of God for you. How can I be so dogmatic? Because God's Word makes it clear:

> Do not be unequally yoked together with unbelievers. For what fellowship has righteousness with lawlessness? And what communion has light with darkness? And what accord has Christ with Belial? Or what part has a believer with an unbeliever? And what agreement has the temple of God with idols? For you are the temple of the living God. As God has said: "I will dwell in them And walk among them. I will be their God, And they shall be My people." Therefore "Come out

from among them And be separate, says the Lord. Do not touch what is unclean, And I will receive you. I will be a Father to you, And you shall be My sons and daughters, Says the Lord Almighty" (2 Cor. 6:14-18).

What fellowship can light have with darkness? What fellowship can the believer have with an unbeliever?

When God sends life's partner your way, there won't be any question. When you talk about Jesus Christ to your prospective mate, Jesus won't be a stranger to him or her. You'll be talking about his or her best friend, too.

"Can two walk together, unless they are agreed?" (Amos 3:3). Unless you both have a relationship with Jesus Christ, there is no unity.

If you decide you will not marry anyone who is not a Christian, you narrow down your choices. If you choose to obey God, you won't even consider dating an unbeliever.

God gave us this principle for our own

good. He wants you to be happy, fulfilled, and living in spiritual unity with the person you choose as your mate for life. You only have to look around to see the heartache a marriage without Christ can bring.

When love is involved, however, some Christian singles fall into the trap of thinking, *I'm going to be God's omnipotent exception.* Then they come to me and ask, "Would you pray with me about marrying so-and-so?"

I reply by asking if the person is a Christian. If they say "No," I answer, "No. I won't pray about it."

"Why not?" they usually ask.

"God has already given you His opinion on the matter: 'Be ye not unequally yoked together with unbelievers.' This decision is not up for discussion, so we don't need to pray about it." Why should I waste my time praying about something God has al-

ready stated is off-limits? It is not God's will for a believer to marry an unbeliever. He has revealed His will in the Word of God.

Occasionally, a sincere Christian young person will say, "Pastor LaHaye, I know you teach that we shouldn't be unequally yoked to unbelievers, but I believe that this time it's different. I'm led of the Holy Spirit."

When I challenge him on it, he responds, "But don't you think I can be led of the Spirit?"

"Yes, I do, but the Bible and the Holy Spirit are never in opposition," I explain. "And God the Holy Spirit will never lead you contrary to what He has written in His Word."

Happy is the individual who decides to go God's way in all things.

I don't care how blonde her hair, how fast his sports car, how great her personality, or how big his income — if he or she is not a believer, you — as a Christian — have no business marrying him or her.

As a pastor, I will not, under any circumstances, marry a couple if one is an unbeliever.

Why am I so dogmatic about not marrying a couple who will be unequally yoked? Because I've never seen it work out for the good of either partner. In fact, the result is usually a marriage of heartache at best and divorce at worst.

Years ago, a beautiful young woman named Linda came to my office. "Pete and I want to get married," she told me, her face glowing. "We've been engaged for nine months. Would you perform the ceremony?"

"Well, is he a Christian?" I asked.

"He's a different faith, but we always go to church together."

"How is that?" I asked skeptically.

"We go to his church early, and then come to my church late," she replied sweetly.

I wanted to tell her that this kind of arrangement may work while you are dating, but I doubted that it would continue — especially after they had children. One partner would have to choose.

Instead, I said, "No, Linda, I won't marry you because it's unscriptural."

We hassled about it a while, and she vacillated back and forth until she finally resolved to submit her decision to the Lord.

She prayed, "Lord, if you don't want me to marry Pete, I won't marry him."

Within a few weeks, she lost interest in him.

Several years later, I received a letter from Linda in which she thanked me for the counsel I had given her that day. "I am now married to a Christian husband and we have one child," she wrote.

What happened to Pete? "Pete has been married and divorced twice," she wrote, "within a three-year period. I'm so glad I listened to your advice."

The day I counseled Linda, I gave her this suggestion: "We have in our church 36 women and 4 men who are married to unsaved partners. I'll give you their names and phone numbers, and you can call any of them and ask, 'If you had it to do over again, would you marry an unbeliever?' Out of those 40 people, not one of them would answer yes."

In spite of God's grace and the love He can give through a difficult situation, it never pays to disobey God's Word.

When God's man or God's woman comes

your way, you won't have to wonder or question God's will. He or she will come wrapped in so much Christian packaging that there will be no doubt. Then for the rest of your life, you will be able to say, "Every good gift and every perfect gift is from above" (James 1:17).

Don't settle for less than God's good and perfect will for you.

2. Don't confuse sexual attraction for love.

All of us have a physical, magnetic attraction toward certain people. Just as an electromagnet can draw steel to itself, certain types of individuals of the opposite sex attract us more than others. It doesn't really have anything to do with looks, and many people in our society confuse this for love.

Suppose we numbered people — from one to ten — according to this strange, biological magnetic attraction. If you are a five, and you find yourself in close proximity to somebody of your number, your senses come to life. You perceive that someone nearby is on your same wavelength.

After couples are married, the idealists think, *Oh, there's just one person in the world I can be drawn to like that.* Christian psychologist Dr. Henry Brandt has said you could have this magnetic attraction for probably one million people of the opposite sex within your own three-year age bracket in America alone.

If that many of the opposite sex are on your wavelength, they can't all be the one person God has chosen for you. What is it then? Plain old biological, magnetic attraction. While this phenomenon may generate momentary excitement, it also creates many tempting problems.

You could work together for years in the same office with a person of the opposite sex and not be polarized toward him or her in the least. But let a new employee come on the scene who's on your same wavelength, and right away you've got problems.

I once had a secretary who was not only quite beautiful but very personable and outgoing. Whenever other pastors would come into the office, they would walk in and — before they would sit down I'd know exactly what they were going to say: "Good night, LaHaye! How does your wife let you have a secretary like that?"

To tell the truth, I was surprised myself! Actually, I considered her more like a sister, and we worked together well for two years. Why? Because we weren't on the same wavelength.

I'll be honest. That has not been true of all the secretaries I've ever had, or all the women who have ever come into my office.

Where the opposite sex is concerned, I have always maintained a hands-off relationship. The Bible says, "avoid the very appearance of evil," and "make no provision for the flesh." Happy is the man who knows the extent and the inclinations of his flesh and makes no provision for it.

Most marriages in America today result from one dominating force — sexual attraction. Inevitably, these couples wake up one day to the fact they have almost nothing else in common. Then, someone new — who's on the same wavelength — comes along, ignites that fire, and the process starts all over again. No wonder there are so many divorces and remarriages in our country.

Unless Jesus Christ is at the center of your marriage, the hope of a happy and lasting relationship is nearly impossible.

"How can I avoid making the mistake of being drawn to the wrong person?" you ask.

Whenever God brings you together with the right person, he or she will be the same number you are. If you're a ten, then

you don't want a six. He or she will also be on the same spiritual wavelength, and you will enjoy unity in Christ.

3. Avoid marrying under pressure.

Over the years, I have counseled with more than one young woman who was distraught over the condition of her marriage.

After pouring out her heart, I couldn't help but ask, "Why in the world did you marry him in the first place?"

"I was unhappy at home. My father was making life miserable for me. This nice guy offered me security, so I married him."

When a young man or woman comes from an unhappy home, he or she may see marriage as a way of escape.

A fellow may be tired of his dominating parents and decide that marriage would be a nice way out. A girl who is insecure about her father's love may seek a husband to fulfill the affection she's missing at home.

If you're miserable where you are, a change of circumstance won't make you happy.

God is able to give you joy in your present situation or open another door for you. Marriage, however, should never be used as an escape ladder.

Don't let the devil tell you that if you don't marry so and so, he'll get away from you — or if you don't marry Susie quickly, somebody else will grab her. Well, if he's so intemperate and undependable, then you don't want him. If your love isn't strong enough to hold her, is it going to be improved by marriage?

Besides, if she is God's girl for you, she's in the net — your net. Now you don't know it, and she doesn't know it, but God knows.

Girls, you don't have to panic. You can just keep playing cat and mouse with him until he catches you. Let him brag to all his friends how he popped the question. It's important to make him think he did it all and that you were just the innocent bystander.

Relax and take your time. Enjoy the dating game. If you're not in a hurry, you are more likely to make the right decision. Panic palace is a dreadful place to live, and decisions made under pressure are disastrous. God is not in a hurry.

If you're in love with someone and you think he or she is the person, then commit that person to God and give the relationship time. Let it simmer.

As a pastor, I have an unconditional rule concerning mar-

riages. I will not, under any circumstances, officiate at the wedding unless the two people have gone together for six months — and that's the barest minimum.

Why? Because if you haven't gone with a person with the intention of marriage for six months, you don't really know him or her. I've had this rule long enough to have saved a number of couples from a disastrous experience.

One young lady often stops after church to shake my hand and whisper, "Thank you."

I know why she's so grateful.

She had been dating a young man for only two months and wanted to get married in the church.

I told her, "I can't because you two haven't been going together for six months. And if I don't officiate at the wedding, you can't use the church for the ceremony."

"Okay, we'll wait," she agreed reluctantly.

About the fourth month, she and her fiancé had a big fight and broke up. Within a short time she met and fell in love with Mr.

Right. Now they have two children.

Every now and then, she tells me, "I'm so glad I waited for God's man."

4. Test your love by separation.

I'm thoroughly convinced that every serious relationship should be tested by a long period of separation.

Sometimes a young man will go off to school or join the military or take a job that separates him from his girlfriend for several months or a year. When this happens, it gives both a chance to view their relationship more re-alistically without the constant pressure of dating.

If it is impossible to separate geographically, a couple could decide to re-frain from contact for a month or six weeks. During the time of separation, they can assess their true feelings.

When a couple is dating on a regular basis — day after day or week after week — it is difficult to be objective about their relationship. A crucial decision like marriage requires an unbiased, almost analytical process.

During this period of separation — or at some point in your relationship — you need to make sure you are in the center of God s will and that this is the person He wants for you.

5. Learn how to resolve disagreements.

If you and the person you are courting are in constant disunity over minor and major issues, look out!

Some people think arguing is a fact of life between partners — whether they are dating, engaged, or married. Many marriage counselors believe that occasional quarrels between couples are good since they help "clear the air."

A University of Michigan team of doctors discovered, however, that habitual quarrels can impair the health of both partners, increasing the risk of arthritis in wives and ulcers in husbands. These two illnesses seem to arise more frequently in couples who consistently argue, bicker, and quarrel with each other.

A young couple who was experiencing conflict in their relationship, came to me for counseling. "Arguing helps us keep issues out in the open," they told me.

I responded with this question: "How should you — as spirit-filled Christians — view arguing?"

When they couldn't come up with a response, I said, "Any time you raise your voice or get enraged, you're not being controlled by the Holy Spirit; you're being controlled by anger motivated by selfishness."

Then I gave them three suggestions:

A. Back off from any heated discussions.

"Wait until you can let your emotions be controlled by the Spirit," I told them.

"Isn't it more harmful to keep our emotions bottled up inside?" the young man asked.

"No," I replied. "Arguing seldom has a productive outcome."

B. Don't refuse to talk.

Learn to discuss issues without letting your emotions get the best of you. Productive discussion cannot take place in an atmosphere of anger.

The Bible says, "Speak the truth in love."

You don't have to argue and quarrel. You can lovingly

WHEN YOU
DWELL ON THE
WEAKNESSES OF
YOUR PARTNER
RATHER THAN
THEIR STRENGTHS,
YOU OVERLOOK
THE STRENGTHS
THAT ATTRACTED
YOU TO THEM IN
THE FIRST PLACE —
AND YOUR LOVE
BEGINS TO DIE.

Beverly LaHaye

discuss as the Holy Spirit leads.

C. Don't let arguing become a habit.

If you work on this area now — before marriage — you can keep arguing from becoming a habitual problem. If, on the other hand, the conflicts in your relationship cannot be resolved without anger, any marriage plans should be put on hold.

Don't marry anyone who cannot control his or her emotions. Unbridled anger can lead to mental and physical abuse.

One day I found myself counseling a distraught, 97-pound woman and her 290-pound athletic husband.

"How did you get that bruise under your eye?" I asked the wife.

Looking down, the husband answered for her. "Preacher, I hate to admit this, but I did that. It was all my fault."

"No," she interrupted. "It was my fault. I pushed him to do it."

"Why would a woman tempt a big guy like him?" I asked.

"I got so angry I couldn't control myself," she sobbed.

As I counseled this couple, I told them what I'm telling you: Anger will put you out of control. When you're angry, you will always make bad decisions — and bad decisions always result in negative consequences.

"It's dangerous for a player to get angry," a football player told me, "because he makes himself vulnerable to serious injury."

This defensive back went on to explain: "Whenever you see us walking back up the field with the wide receiver who's gone down for a pass, what do you think we're saying? We're not inviting him for lunch the next day. We're trying to needle him and make him so mad that he can't make a good, mental decision on the next play." Anger can cause you to make dangerous decisions.

A 19 year old on the junior college football team had never gotten a traffic ticket when he took off speeding down the San Diego three-decker freeway. As his car went around the corner — where a sign said "slow to 40 miles an hour" — he hit the curve at 95 miles an hour. The centrifugal force took him up over the small guardrail and his car nose-dived into the concrete. He was killed instantly.

The officer investigating the accident learned that seven minutes before this young man died, he had backed out of his

girlfriend's driveway that Saturday morning, squealed his tires for 105 feet, and was dead in seven minutes. Why? Because he and his girlfriend had an argument.

You say, "What a fool."

He really wasn't a fool — just a short-term fool. But that's all it takes. One short-term burst of anger can end a relationship — or a life.

6. Make sure you have the same life goals.

As a couple, you don't have to share everything and you don't have to be exactly alike, but most of your interests should be similar. This is why both partners should be vitally interested in serving Christ.

If you're interested in winning souls and walking the spirit-filled life, don't be satisfied with anyone who isn't. Don't say, "Oh, I'll change him after we're married." Forget it.

The best time to change him or her is before marriage. If the person you are dating is not subject to change, you are taking a huge risk that could compromise your own walk with the Lord.

When my wife and I were dating at college, I became friendly with her older sister, Barrie, who was also a student.

One day, as I was walking Barrie to her dorm, I said, "I notice you and Bill are seeing a lot of each other. Is your relationship getting serious?"

"Well, I don't know," Barrie answered softly. "You see a few years ago, God spoke to me. And I believe He wants me to be a missionary to the Chinese."

"Oh, that's interesting," I replied — although at the time I didn't even know what a missionary was!

About two weeks later, Bill and I were crossing the campus together, and I said, "Hey, man. You look like you're really intrigued with Barrie. Are you thinking of getting married?"

"Yes, I am," he answered in his usual serious tone.

"When are you going to pop the question?" I asked bluntly. This topic of conversation intrigued me since I had already made up my mind I was going to ask Beverly to marry me.

"Well, I've got another question to ask her first," Bill answered.

"What is it?"

He responded, "When I was in the infantry I was stationed at a base in Texas. My bunkmate was Nate Saint, one of the five missionaries martyred in South America among the Acca Indi-

ans. Nate was a unique Christian. I'd never met anyone like him in my life. He was committed to reaching the lost for Christ, and he knew his military training was preparing him to serve the Lord on the mission field. The Holy Spirit used Nate in my life. Since then, God has called me to be a missionary among the Chinese."

I didn't know what to say, so I kept my big mouth shut.

Bill continued, "Before I ask Barrie to marry me, I've got to ask her what God wants to do with her life."

A few days later, I saw Bill floating across the campus, and I knew he had gotten the right answer to both his questions.

Several years ago, our congregation sent my wife and me on a trip to visit our church's missionaries. Over the years, I've seen some very productive ministries, but I was amazed when we visited Bill and Barrie and saw what they had accomplished in Taiwan.

At that time, they were ministering in areas where there was no gospel witness and nothing but raw paganism. One place was so committed to demonic worship, we could feel the power of the devil.

In one predominately Buddhist town of 40,000 people, however, I had the joy of preaching to 125 born-again believers whom Barrie and Bill had led to Christ. Today there are three other churches in Taiwan among the Chinese people — each with a native pastor whom Bill led to Christ and discipled through Bible school.

Recently their first church invited them to the 25th anniversary of its founding. One thousand people attended!

Barrie and Bill found not only God's vocation for their lives — they found God's mate for the ministry to which He had called them. Needless to say, they have a storybook marriage.

Whatever your vocation, that's the kind of marriage I hope you enjoy with the mate God gives you.

7. Determine if your personalities complement each other.

Are you strong where he is weak, and is he strong where you are weak? You'll find that opposites attract each other.

When gregarious George Sanguine arrives at a party, he invigorates the room with his outgoing personality and lively conversation. Everyone notices him — he makes a point of that.

Quiet Susie Melancholy, on the other hand, spends the evening sitting in a corner, looking sweet and demure. She never

does anything to draw attention to herself, never says anything wrong, and always laughs at the right time.

All the while, she's admiring George Sanguine and his outgoing, uninhibited manner. Susie thinks, "Oh, what a great guy."

After the party, as George speeds home in his big car — everything he does is big and fast — he talks to himself.

"George, why can't you learn to keep your big mouth shut" he says out loud. "You dominated the whole conversation. Why can't you be like Susie Melancholy. You know, she's so reserved and pretty. She must be smart, too. After all, she laughed at all my jokes. I think I'll give her a call."

As Susie arrives home in her little Geo Metro, she thinks, *What a wonderful guy George is. He's so different from me. If I weren't so shy, maybe he would have shown more interest.*

Suddenly, her phone rings.

"Susie, I noticed you at the party tonight,"

George begins.

"Oh," she answers, "were you there?"

"How about supper tomorrow night?"

"Well, hold the phone just a moment. I'll check my date book."

After shuffling around for a few moments, she returns to the phone and says, "Well, George, I do have an opening tomorrow night."

They go out for dinner, and after a whirlwind courtship, they marry and — with George in charge — take off on an emotionally super-charged honeymoon.

This marriage is based on need — and that's good because we need each other. Don't marry someone who doesn't need you. You need to be needed. Every living, breathing human being needs someone else.

After the honeymoon, however, George and Susie discover

that the subconscious differences that attracted them to each other are accompanied by certain weaknesses.

The day after the honeymoon, they are back in her apartment. They chose to live at her place because his was in a shambles.

The next morning, George wakes up bright-eyed and bushy-tailed — as sanguines usually do. He's in the shower singing away, and Susie is still in a fog. (Melancholys are not early birds.)

When she hears all this racket, Susie realizes she is a wife! Catapulting out of bed, she throws on her perfectly folded robe and begins to make breakfast. George whips through the kitchen just in time for her to present the first burnt offering.

They say their sweet goodbyes, and Susie stumbles back into the bedroom — and the moment of truth.

Her once well-ordered bedroom is a shambles. Susie hadn't noticed it when they went to bed, but he just threw his pants over the chair and his coat on the floor and wadded up his socks next to the bed. And lo and behold, there's a wet towel in the middle of the bed!

In the bathroom, the sink is filled with beard chips and the bath mat is sopping wet. The contents of the medicine cabinet are in a shambles from his hunt for the hair spray — and he didn't even put the cap back on! To make matters worse, he squeezed the toothpaste in the middle of the tube and used her toothbrush on his teeth!

Suddenly, Susie realizes she has an adjustment to make.

It doesn't matter if the man is the melancholy and the woman is the sanguine or vice versa. Whatever the personality types, adjustments have to be made.

If you know beforehand the type of person you are marrying, you will be able to anticipate the differences in your temperaments and lifestyles. If you focus on your partner's strengths and make adjustments for his or her weaknesses, you will have a long, happy marriage.

8. Commit your relationship to the Lord.

If your relationship is spiritually deteriorating, look out! You are walking on dangerous ground — and this happens more often than not. Couples often get more interested in each other than they do in the will of God.

You should be attending church together, praying when you go out on dates, and encouraging one another in your walk with the Lord.

Never get to the place where you're willing to say, "Lord, I want him or her, no matter what!" That's the prayer for disaster.

Happy is the young person who is willing to pray, "Lord, I commit my relationship with him or her to you." Commit your way and the person you love to the Lord.

Always be honest with God. If you love someone, tell God about it. Say, "Lord, I love so-and-so. And I want to commit that love to You. If You want it to come to fruition, then You just increase my love. If You don't, then squelch it."

God is the author of love, and He can change your emotions if you submit them to Him. This is where a period of separation can help you assess the situation reasonably.

Then, when you do make a decision, you'll have that peace that passes all understanding.

9. Wait for God's best.

There are probably many people in this world to whom you could be happily married. But there is only one person who is God's best for you.

If you let the Lord make the final decision, you will never have to wonder about your choice of a mate. You will always know that your marriage was ordained by God.

When I first met Steve and his fiancée, their two-year relationship was already stormy.

Although he had been planning to be a history professor, Steve felt that God was calling him to preach the gospel. He had recently changed his major at college and was studying for the ministry.

His fiancée, an ambitious graduate student, appeared to be the dominant one in their relationship. In fact, she could chew him up and spit him out — and they weren't even married!

I couldn't help but think that the last thing this tender young man needed was a wife with more education and a more forceful personality than he had. His perfectionist temperament was already suffering.

Together, the three of us prayed about their relationship. I suggested they commit it to God and say, "Lord, if You want us to marry, then increase our love; and if You don't want us to marry, cause it to die."

Before I knew it, the engagement was off.

About the same time, a beautiful, outgoing young lady came to me for counseling.

"I've been dating an airline pilot," she told me. "Tom is a Christian, but we don't share the same commitment. I really want to serve the Lord, but he's more drawn to the things of the world."

"Just being equally yoked with a believer is not enough," I told her. "If you want Jesus Christ to use your life, you don't want to saddle yourself with a carnal Christian. You want a Christian who is on your level spiritually — someone motivated to move out for God."

That day she prayed the same prayer as the ministerial student and his fiancée had prayed: "Lord, if You don't want me to marry Tom just take away the feeling I have."

Sure enough, something happened, and the feelings died.

One Sunday morning, as I was seated behind the pulpit getting ready to preach, I noticed Steve, the young ministerial student, about eight rows back. Just at that moment, one of the ushers brought in the lovely young lady who had been dating the airline pilot and seated her right next to him.

When I saw them sitting there together, I looked up and said, "Heavenly Father, did You notice that?"

I'm almost certain I heard God say, "Who do you think arranged it all, anyway?"

My young friend was sharp enough to know he was sitting next to a quality creature. Before she got out the door, he found out where she lived.

Soon they were going together, and every time the church doors were open they were there. They were on the same spiritual level and had many common interests. Her outgoing, vivacious ways complemented his low-key, reserved manner.

When they came to talk to me about setting the wedding date, everything fit. They waited even longer than the six-month period.

I'll never forget their wedding day as long as I live.

About an hour before the wedding, I found her dressed in her gown with the veil flowing out behind and passing out corsages to the wedding party.

I found Steve in the back of the church, pacing up and down, with beads of perspiration on his face.

When everyone was finally in place, she came floating down the aisle. I could tell from the look on his face that there wasn't another person in the church as far as he was concerned.

At the end of the ceremony, I always have the couple bow for prayer at the kneeling bench. When I reached over and put my hands on theirs, I prayed. Then the soloist started to sing "The Lord's Prayer."

When I looked at this brilliant young man with his gifted temperament, I saw tears streaking down his face. She had her eyes closed with a great big smile on her face.

About halfway through the solo, she opened her eyes and saw him wiping tears off his chin. He didn't want to use the handkerchief in the tuxedo, and he didn't have another handkerchief. She quickly sized up the situation, reached down inside her dress for a tissue, and handed it to him.

He took it, wiped his tears, handed it back to her, and she popped it back in her gown. She noticed I had watched the whole thing, so she gave me a wink and one of her vivacious smiles. I knew that couple would make it — and they have. They have joyfully served their Lord together for over 20 years.

Now if there is a moral to that story, it is this: Give God a chance to bring you His best.

Allow me to pray for you:

Heavenly Father, may the young person reading this book not settle for second-rate, but find Your perfect will for life's vocation and a life's partner.

We ask this in the name of Jesus Christ, who loved us so much that He literally gave himself for us. Amen.

DISCOUNT COUPON

Save $10 on your

Personalized Temperament Analysis

- Discover your personality type for only $15 (that's $10 off the regular price) and enjoy the benefits of knowing yourself better.
- To receive your personalized temperament analysis, fill in the information below and send it with your check for $15 to:

Family Life Seminars
P.O. Box 2700
Washington, DC 20013-2700

Name_____

Address_____

City_____

State _____Zip_____